WAVES

poems on grief

GLORIA EID

DEDICATION

to grieving hearts

living in the nuance of keeping it together
when things have fallen apart

~ for Papi ~

DEAR READER,

I wonder about you. I wonder about who left you holding this book in your hands. I wonder how many days they've been the first thought in your head upon waking, and whether you've already lived that first surprising morning where they weren't. I wonder if that day stunned you, too.

I wonder about what you remember and perhaps what you've tried to forget. I wonder about their voice, what it sounds like, and that thing they always said. I wonder about the song that heals you and whether you've let yourself dance again.

I wonder whether you, too, have found yourself washing dishes in the kitchen one average afternoon and, in a blink, sobbing tears into the sink. I wonder about all the other odd moments when your waves of grief roll in: on the bus; in the restaurant; on the toilet; in a gym class.

I know how challenging it can feel everyday to stay in your heart when it aches to be there. But there is nothing else required; nothing more to achieve. Because what else is there for a grieving person to do but to grieve?

I can't ever know what your hurt hurts like, how painful your pain is, or whether your love feels like mine, but I do know that you are not alone. I hope these poems may connect us. I hope this little book helps you grieve more fully – because to grieve fully is to live fully – and my greatest hope is that you allow your grief to support you now, and for the rest of time, in living your life fully alive.

Gloria

CONTENTS

PROLOGUE

Moments were measured
only in breaths.

Time ceased to matter.

Even the intervals
between your exhales
felt

infinite.

I would match the rhythm
of my breath
to yours

Watching your chest
for hours,
wondering if

there would be one more
moment

to measure.

AND NOW

And it was at that age
the artist arrived
in search of me.
Asked me to be The One for Words.

She summoned me
into an ocean of deep blue waters,
never minding I had not learned
how to swim.

But that was the point, it seemed:

Her underworld I could not access
unless I unclipped from my own preserving;
until I slid one arm out
of the jacket I wore that kept me afloat

and then my other arm.

And once I did, I sunk
into an air thicker than this sky I knew.

Before this, there was only distance.

She was a stranger who compelled me
with a curiosity that
I could not think away.

And so I drowned,
leaving bubbles at the waves.

Died

to discover new life
in the depths of her
blue waters.

LOVING IN LOSS

Purple was the colour of the shirt
I dressed you in.
Sent you over into mystery
looking ever classy,
balancing the dullness
of your pale and greying skin.

If your spirit were a colour now,
I think it would be purple;
purple like this journal
that I'm writing you in.

A purple vivid and sharp
a purple soft and aglow;
I keep your spirit dressed now
in all of these tones.

NEW NORMAL

I begin today
and every day forward
in what I've been told
will be my new normal.

BREATHE AND

Breathe   and go slowly.
Learn from the trees
who lose their leaves this time of year
and still stand
unworried.

Breathe and go swiftly.
Look to the birds
who sit on branches
unconcerned how strong their branch is
for they only need their wings to fly.

Breathe
and go steady.
Look to the moon who,
       after nights of shining
       in only crescent linings,
eventually has her time to shine
in full.

STARSEED VACATION

I'm tired of being so human.
Send me back to the stars.
I need more practice
for the dark.

TOMORROW'S SOIL

Crawl down into the ditch of my pain
and sit with me in it

just long enough
so that I can pull myself back up
and touch the soil of
tomorrow

THESE HANDS

What lies around me, I cannot leave.
I don't know how not
to pay attention to the pieces
of myself
scattered.

My own hands find themselves again
with nothing to do and nowhere to be
but assigned to this body.

My own hands are so lost.

One at a time,
I show them the way home:

A safe place to rest
on top of my heart;
here they lay gently

for what they once loved they cannot hold.

These hands have nothing left
but to find themselves again.

BUT SOMETIMES

People always say it hurts at night
but sometimes it is in the middle
of a bright summer day
and the whiff of fresh cut watermelon
will send the shivers to my
bones.

I smell you
in the juiciest fruits
I pick at the market
and when the scent of freshly peeled orange
lingers in the picnic air,
I think of you.

I will always see you in the carrots
of every colour.

They say it hurts at night,
but sometimes
it's at the brink of dusk
on a walk
around the block

when the scent of wet evening grass
from a neighbour with her garden hose
sends me back to our lawn.

I stop
and watch her water
in peace;
I inhale
to a time
when everything
was simple.

MADE OF

I hope you get to hold your broken pieces one day and delight in the edges you're made of.

A SPACE

For the times when you have nothing to say –

there is a space for the wordless.

THE DESERT

Alone in the desert,
there is no truth to question.

The heavy sandwinds blow you over
and though the crystals
scratch your skin,
you make a blanket
of them.

No one finds you here,
in the desert, covered
in silence.

They don't know
how to hear you
when you're quiet and
free.

HOPING

I am hoping
to be strong enough
to stay conscious
through this teaching —

of life and loss and grieving.

SEESAW

Only one hundred and twenty
days
already;
only, already;

how time seesaws between an instant
and
eternity.

. . .

The most consistent thing I've done
in my life so far is think
of my dad.

Mostly, of those moments that hurt
to remember but are hard
to forget,
etched into that timeless place of
vivid memory.

But even still, after a while,
  there has become more space between them,
more care for what remains,
  more mind to give to the eternal,
more breath
  for that which does not die.

. . .

Today I walked and walked and
walked and walked —
wandering, wondering.

Thankful for the clear blue sky and the cool breeze.
Thankful to have had sunglasses
instead of the
umbrella.

THE MIDDLE

When you find yourself in the middle
of what was and what will be
admire this space in between.

There is a life there;
a bold invitation
to stay awhile

in that place
that does not ask you
to rush

that does not need you
to know

that does not want you
to be so quick to go.

There is a gift there,
in the middle
of what was and what will be

because the most alive life
there is for us
is in
the in-between.

WORLD SHUT DOWN

It all flipped on its head
overnight,
and it was chaos
and quiet
at once.

I couldn't help but feel as though in some way,
I had been here before:

    Thrust into a void.
Sense of purpose and
direction shaken
and stirred. Normal
di
  ssol
     ve
       d.

I understood these sensations,
this confusion, this
uprooting.

I remembered the unexpected invitation
to reassess my life.

THE GREATEST TASK

When parts of yourself feel fractured
and when what was real is not-real
anymore,
the greatest task
is to try to love
the questions you now have

that you never
wanted
to ask.

To try to be unthreatened by them
and by what
you don't know.

To be in love with life
while in pain with life

and to find ways to keep your heart
o p e n
when it makes more sense
to close.

PARADOX OF MOURNING

Whispers of peace
tap lightly
on a pounding drum
of grief

to guide me.

Small waves of comfort
spill softly
into an ocean
of this rage

inside me.

SOMETHING

Having something
to look forward to
– a visit, event, trip –
does not fix anything;

but
it helps to remind you
in your grief
that you are still
alive.

THE 13TH GUEST

No one expects me to bring
a 13th guest, not even me

but somehow I arrive
with the unwelcomed gift
of destiny
weighing on me;
an unfestive presence of
death
disturbing the party.

Its shadow enters the most
alive spaces and

when it exits, it carries out
the thickness of everything
unsaid by us.

I polarize
inadvertently;

no choice but to direct you
awkwardly

to the 13th guest,
unsettled and tense,

you can't know to expect
the softness
that comes next:

She speaks
with the gift
of honesty;

an invitation
to her kind
of party.

IN COMPANY

Thank you for staying because
the darkness would be darker alone.

And the light —
it's so much brighter when
you're with me.

MAY AGAIN

It's May and I'm sorry.
I may not have
a smile on
that matches the bright sun
out today —
it's shining.

Inside today, I'm crying
at the weight of love
that I can't see.

May is the way it looks to let it all be.

Under its clear skies
I wipe my wet eyes
blurred by the love I can't
touch or hear.

It's May and I'm sorry.
I still turn to the sun when it's blinding
and these flowers get watered
with my tears.

CARNATION INCARNATE

I'm tired of being so human;
please return me to a seed.

Please let me root
and please plant me deep.

For when I grow into a flower,
I'll know how to sway in the wind.

But don't cut me,
don't cut me; I'm still
asking to live

just with soft pistils
as my eyes
and strong leaves
as my limbs.

LETTER FROM GRIEF

I don't know if anyone else
has said this to you before but:
I just want to know what's in your heart.

I know it seems that I've
shown up out of nowhere
and I admit I pop in
without warning
but my promise is:
I'm only here to help.

I can't apologize for who I am.
I know I make you feel like you're losing
your mind or going numb; yes,
I am a unique kind of friend.

Intimidating, at first —
until you rest into my warmth,
my innocence,
my love of you.

I'm here to show you
how to keep going, with new eyes
and new life, and a heart
that stays beating
through repair.

FOR YOU

In case you didn't know:
      the sun shined for you today
and the leaves breathed
a little bit greener
and the rain washed away
the sidewalk chalk
because you mustn't look down anyway.

      The sea made ripples
to thank you for your multiple
smiles.

The birds chirp
at your every laugh
(their way of encouragement).

In case you didn't know:
      you are loved.

Look to the sun the leaves the rain
the sea the birds
      they will remind you.

WHEN THE WORST HAPPENS

When we have things working out for us
the way we want them to,
it's easy to name what we're grateful for.
Even when life feels hard and disorienting,
most of the time, things can always be worse.

But, what about when the worst happens?
When someone you love dies?
When you are the saddest you've ever been?
Where do you find gratitude in that?

First: You seriously don't. In the name of Love, you won't.

First, you wail in despair, by yourself,
or in the company of someone who happens to
check in on you that dark day. You find nothing else
important for a while. You wonder when you will
feel better again, and that idea seems
impossible for a while.

You have no concept of time for a while.
You do not know whether it is bright or dark outside,
because it makes no difference for a while.
You do not consider whether there is any food
in the fridge because you are not eating
for a while.

You do not want your bed because you
are not sleeping for a while and
it is where your sadness lies
awake with you.
You want to forget it for a while.

You do not go looking for pain,
but it is all you can see and feel for a while.

And so, you need to have
a space to scream
for as long as your vocal chords will vibrate.
You need a bucket for your tears;
a hair tie to keep the sweat off your neck —
(grief is an exercise of a silent strength)
and you will learn that you break more
than a sweat.

You break your plates.
You break the hinges off your cupboards.
You break the promises you never could have kept.
You break the dawn, wide-eyed and sleep-deprived.

If you were to go looking for pain,
there's no way you wouldn't find it.

But then —
there comes a moment when the
wave you're caught in breaks.

And you are not left with many options
but to be pushed
  towards a shoreline.

Eventually, your emotions
(your energy in motion)
take you back to a place of safety where you can
breathe again for a while,
to a place where you are swept
back to some familiar ground.

Once you notice that where you are feels
less painful,
here is where you can be grateful
for a relief.

You are spared a bit of time before the next
wave crashes to go looking
for something else. Look for it.

Call out to the simplest truths that
you know exist with or without your grief.
You will find kindness there
and it is only kindness that makes sense
after a while.

In the darkest times,
bring your heart and mind back to the basics;

gratitude doesn't have to be grandiose.

I'm grateful for...

Not denying my pain.
For having feelings.
For friendship, and solitude,
for music, and walks,
for family, for FaceTime,
and hugs, for
poetry,
breathing,
for knowing love.

Be kind to your sad self.
Look for something
that offers you even a moment
of peace and comfort
among the bouts the stings the stabs and the waves
of your grieving.

You will find kindness there
and kindness is everywhere if you look for it.

NOTES

But Sometimes

poem title and line "people always say it hurts at night" inspired from *On Missing Them* by Rose Scanlan

The 13th Guest

title inspired from refugeingrief.com Writing Your Grief course prompt #13

When The Worst Happens

spoken word featured in Healing Through Poetry - Episode 3 - Living Inside Grief documentary series, sponsored by TELUS STORYHIVE and directed by Garima Soni, available on YouTube

line "be kind to your sad self" inspired from *Let me be to my sad self hereafter kind* by Peter Pouncey, Rules for Old Men Waiting: A Novel

line "and it is only kindness that makes sense anymore" inspired from *Kindness* by Naomi Shihab Nye, from The Words Under the Words: Selected Poems

ABOUT THE AUTHOR

Gloria is a writer, poet, life & leadership coach and grief guide who helps people navigate their growth and transitions, access their creative abilities, and become who they need to be to carry out their unique roles in life and career.

Through her own experiences with grief and death, and her fascination with life on earth, her work often explores how to find peace in life's mysteries, carry onward in the aftermath of change and loss, and live in the nuance of keeping it together when things have fallen apart.

Her coaching and writing is known to help others transform self-doubt into self-trust, lead from love, and live their truth.

You can find out more about her and her work at www.gloriaeid.com.

Made in the USA
Coppell, TX
25 November 2024

41026807R00030